DISCOVER!

AMERICA'S AMAZING LANDMARKS

THE STATUE OF LIBERTY

By Marie Roesser

Enslow PUBLISHING

Please visit our website, www.enslow.com. For a free color catalog of all our high-quality books, call toll free 1-800-398-2504 or fax 1-877-980-4454.

Library of Congress Cataloging-in-Publication Data
Names: Roesser, Marie, author.
Title: The Statue of Liberty / Marie Roesser.
Description: New York : Enslow Publishing, [2026] | Series: America's amazing landmarks | Includes bibliographical references and index.
Identifiers: LCCN 2024061911 (print) | LCCN 2024061912 (ebook) | ISBN 9781978544079 (library binding) | ISBN 9781978544062 (paperback) | ISBN 9781978544086 (ebook)
Subjects: LCSH: Statue of Liberty (New York, N.Y.)–Juvenile literature. | New York (N.Y.)–Buildings, structures, etc.–Juvenile literature.
Classification: LCC F128.64.L6 R635 2026 (print) | LCC F128.64.L6 (ebook) | DDC 974.7/1–dc23/eng/20250207
LC record available at https://lccn.loc.gov/2024061911
LC ebook record available at https://lccn.loc.gov/2024061912

Portions of this work were originally authored by Siobhan Moriarty and published as *Visit the Statue of Liberty*. All new material this edition authored by Marie Roesser.

Published in 2026 by
Enslow Publishing
2544 Clinton Street
Buffalo, NY 14224

Cover Designer: Nicholas Switalski
Interior Designer: Rachel Rising
Editor: Therese Shea

Photo credits: Cover Xavier MARCHANT/Shutterstock.com; cover, pp. 1, 3-24 Jeffery Edwards/Shutterstock.com; cover, p. 1, 5, 7, 9, 11, 13, 15, 17, 19, 21 Oleksandr Poliashenko/Shutterstock.com; p. 4 RadoPL/Shutterstock.com; p. 5 Peter Hermes Furian/Shutterstock.com; p. 7 https://commons.wikimedia.org/wiki/File:First_meeting_of_Washington_and_Lafayette,_Currier_and_Ives_1876.jpg; p. 9 Fotografie-Hake/Shutterstock.com; pp. 10 (both), 13 Library of Congress; p. 11 Cincila/Shutterstock.com; p. 12 Jose Luis Stephens/Shutterstock.com; p.14 https://commons.wikimedia.org/wiki/File:Richard_Morris_Hunt.jpg; p.15 Zack Frank/Shutterstock.com; p. 17 Igor Link/Shutterstock.com; p. 19 iofoto/Shutterstock.com; p. 20 GagliardiPhotography/Shutterstock.com; p. 21 Domingo Saez/Shutterstock.com.

Printed in the United States of America

Some of the images in this book illustrate individuals who are models. The depictions do not imply actual situations or events.

CPSIA compliance information: Batch #CSENS26: For further information contact Enslow Publishing, at 1-800-398-2504.

CONTENTS

BOLDFACE WORDS APPEAR IN THE GLOSSARY.

A POWERFUL SYMBOL

The Statue of Liberty is a **symbol** of the United States, just as the American flag is. The statue stands on an island in New York Harbor. But it wasn't made in America. The Statue of Liberty came from France.

THE STATUE OF LIBERTY IS COVERED IN THE METAL COPPER. IT WAS A REDDISH-BROWN COLOR BEFORE IT TURNED GREEN!

SIGN OF FRIENDSHIP

During the **American Revolution**, France helped the American **colonies** gain their freedom from Great Britain. Around 1865, French official Édouard de Laboulaye had an idea. He wanted France to create a statue to celebrate the countries' friendship and American liberty, or freedom.

IN THIS PICTURE, GENERAL GEORGE WASHINGTON GREETS A FRENCH SOLDIER NAMED LAFAYETTE.

CHOOSING A SITE

The **sculptor** Frédéric-Auguste Bartholdi was chosen to create the statue. In 1874, Bartholdi sailed to the United States. In New York Harbor, he saw Bedloe's Island. He thought the location would be perfect for a tall statue. Bartholdi began his **design** when he returned to France.

BEDLOE'S ISLAND WAS RENAMED LIBERTY ISLAND IN 1956.

THE DESIGN

Bartholdi designed the statue to look like a Roman goddess. She carries a **torch**. Her crown includes rays of light. The light stood for rays of freedom and **justice** shining out to the world. At her feet are broken chains. These represent the end of slavery in the United States.

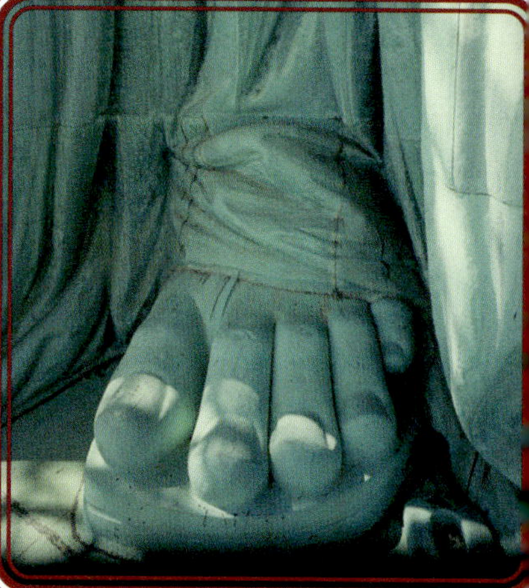

THE STATUE OF LIBERTY HOLDS A TABLET. ON IT IS THE DATE THE **DECLARATION OF INDEPENDENCE** WAS APPROVED.

CONSTRUCTION

The statue has a strong iron frame. Iron bars and steel rods were connected to it. Sheets of copper were hammered to these, to make the "skin."

The statue was designed to move in strong winds instead of being blown over.

Frédéric-Auguste Bartholdi

THE STATUE OF LIBERTY WAS FINISHED IN 1884. IT WAS SHIPPED TO THE UNITED STATES IN PIECES.

An American named Richard Morris Hunt designed the pedestal, or base, for the statue. At the time it was completed, it was the largest concrete structure in the world! In 1886, the statue was put back together on the pedestal.

Richard Morris Hunt

THE REAL NAME OF THE STATUE OF LIBERTY IS "STATUE OF LIBERTY ENLIGHTENING THE WORLD."

A WELCOME SIGHT

Millions of **immigrants** sailed into New York Harbor between 1886 and 1924. To them, the statue was a symbol of welcome. To honor that, a poem called "The New Colossus" was placed in the pedestal in 1903. It says the statue lifts her light to guide immigrants to a new life.

THE POET EMMA LAZARUS WROTE "THE NEW COLOSSUS" IN 1883. A COLOSSUS IS ANOTHER NAME FOR A VERY LARGE STATUE.

NATIONAL MONUMENT

In 1924, the Statue of Liberty was named a national monument. In 1933, the National Park Service began to care for it. Nearby Ellis Island is a part of the Statue of Liberty National Monument as well. Thousands of people visit the Statue of Liberty and Ellis Island each day.

ELLIS ISLAND WAS AN IMMIGRATION STATION FROM 1892 TO 1924.

VISITING THE STATUE

Special boats take visitors to Liberty Island. Tickets are needed to go in the pedestal and up into the crown. Visitors must be ready to climb. There are 192 steps up to the pedestal and another 162 to the crown. The Statue of Liberty is a U.S. symbol you have to see!

VISITORS CAN LOOK OUT WINDOWS IN THE STATUE'S CROWN FOR AN AMAZING VIEW.

GLOSSARY

American Revolution: The war in which the colonies won their freedom from England.

colony: A piece of land under the control of another country.

Declaration of Independence: The piece of writing in which the colonies said they were free from British rule.

design: The pattern or shape of something. Also, to create a pattern or shape.

immigrant: One who comes to a country to settle there.

justice: Fairness.

sculptor: An artist who creates shapes with stone, wood, metal, or other matter.

symbol: Something that stands for something else.

tablet: A flat piece of wood, stone, or metal used for writing.

torch: A stick of wood that is set on fire and carried as a source of light.

FOR MORE INFORMATION

Books

Holdren, Annie C. *Building the Statue of Liberty*. Mankato, MN: Amicus Ink, 2023.

Wilson, Jon. *The Statue of Liberty: A Beacon for Freedom*. Mankato, MN: The Childs World, 2025.

Websites

Statue of Liberty National Monument
www.nps.gov/stli/index.htm
Find out more about how to visit the Statue of Liberty on the National Park Service site.

U.S. History: Statue of Liberty
www.ducksters.com/history/us_1800s/statue_of_liberty.php
Learn other names for the Statue of Liberty and other interesting facts.

Publisher's note to educators and parents: Our editors have carefully reviewed these websites to ensure that they are suitable for students. Many websites change frequently, however, and we cannot guarantee that a site's future contents will continue to meet our high standards of quality and educational value. Be advised that students should be closely supervised whenever they access the internet.

INDEX